START-A-CRAFT

Mask Making

Get started in a new craft with easy-to-follow

projects for beginners

GILL DICKINSON

APPLE

A QUINTET BOOK

Published by The Apple Press
6 Blundell Street
London N7 9BH

ISBN 1-84092-031-9

This book was designed and produced by
Quintet Publishing Limited
6 Blundell Street
London N7 9BH

Creative Director: Richard Dewing
Designer: James Lawrence
Project Editor: Claire Tennant-Scull
Editor: Lydia Darbyshire
Photographer: Andrew Sydenham

Typeset in Great Britain by
Central Southern Typesetters, Eastbourne
Manufactured in Singapore by Eray Scan Pte Ltd
Printed in China by Leefung-Asco Printers Ltd

CONTENTS

INTRODUCTION

As long as people have lived on earth costumes and masks have been made in some form or other, either for decoration or for ceremonial or religious purposes. Masks have been used for dance, theatre, carnivals, celebrations, pagan and religious rituals – or sometimes just for fun and disguise.

The Ancient Greeks were the first to use masks for theatrical performances, and the actors and members of the chorus wore large masks with stylized expressions that could be clearly seen and understood by the audience. We still see traces of these masks in some theatres, which use the outlines of the masks with smiling or sad faces to decorate programmes and foyers. Masks were worn by tribal peoples in West Africa to indicate social position, and the Kalahari tribe made ugly masks to drive away demons. Dragon masks are still used to ward off evil spirits in China.

Carnival is a Christian festival that used to take place in many countries before Lent. Elaborate and beautiful masks and costumes were made for this event, especially in the Caribbean and some South American countries. Venetian masks of the kind inspired in the 16th century by Commedia dell'Arte are still seen today. These simple, traditional masks often take the form of elements such as stars, suns and moon, and half-masks representing characters such as Pierrot, Columbine and Harlequin are used not only in Italy but all around the world.

Whatever form a mask takes, it acts as a disguise. The wearer can act the fool without being recognized or just simply enjoy being another person. In the 18th century, for example, elegant ladies carried masks so that they could flirt with strangers with impunity. Masks can be used today to conjure of an element of menace, mystery or fun.

Even a simple half-mask, quickly made and decorated, can be amusing and fun to wear, while more complicated masks can be used for fancy dress parties or for theatrical performances.

The instructions to make 12 exciting masks are given in this book. They range from the simple to the complicated, from half-masks to full masks that completely cover the face. A variety of media have been used, from papier mâché, fur fabric and feathers to simple masks made from paper plates, while the Monster mask is made from recycled egg cartons. Many of the masks are decorated with pastels or ordinary paints.

MATERIALS AND TECHNIQUES

PAPER AND CARD

Paper is a wonderfully versatile product – it is strong enough to be folded and pleated but it can be torn and cut and then coloured and decorated in dozens of ways. You can also obtain paper and card in a variety of weights and colours.

Paper masks are especially easy for young children to make and they can be as simple or as complicated as you wish. The Seaside Spectacles are an instant, fun disguise made with paper and glue. Paper plates are available in all supermarkets and stationery shops and can be used to make good, strong masks that are light and easy to wear Decorate them imaginatively, and children can do this for themselves using different types of paint and paper.

You can also achieve interesting effects by using coloured paper imaginatively to give a fullness and three-dimensional quality to a mask. The mane of the Lion Mask, for instance, is made from fine strips of paper in a range of shades. Some of the strips are curled with scissors, while others left straight to create an unusually textured, full effect.

PASTEL AND PAINT TECHNIQUES

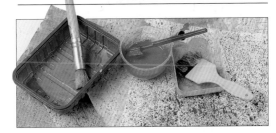

Although paper and card are available in wide ranges of colours and patterns, there will be times when you want to decorate the surface of the mask in a particular way. We have used either poster paints or pastels for the masks described here.

Pastels are used for the Lion Mask and the basic Half-mask. It is best to experiment with pastels on scrap paper to get a feel for how they work. Try using different colours together and try not to apply them too heavily. They will blend more easily if they are used lightly, and you can merge the colours together by rubbing them gently with a finger to create all kinds of shades and textures very quickly When you use pastels, it is a good idea to place a clean sheet of paper over areas that you have already coloured so that you do not smudge the pastels with your hand. You should always use fixative with pastels, which are not stable and quickly smudge and fade.

Poster paints are widely available and they are ideal for children to use. Colours can be mixed on saucers or in old food containers.

You can use all kinds of painting techniques on the masks. Spattering with a brush and old toothbrush was used on the Medusa Mask, for example, and you could also use sponges, rags and, of course, your fingers. For a really rich, deep colour, apply one coat and leave it to dry before you apply a second, or even a third, coat.

PAPIER MÂCHÉ

Making and using papier mâché is both simple and cheap, but it does need more time, because you have to leave the layers to dry out. When it is finished, papier mâché is very light but durable, and it will withstand quite a lot of hard wear. It is a very versatile medium, which we have used to make the Punk Mask, which shows how easy it is to build up a quite complex shape. The Witch is the most time-consuming mask in the book, and it is a project for the real enthusiast, although you could cut the time in half by buying a cheap witch's hat from a joke shop and decorating it.

Once you have made a papier mâché mask or half-mask you can adapt it to all kinds of styles. The Woodland Half-mask could be adapted for different projects, for example – perhaps to look like an animal or even a simple painted Venetian-style mask. Making papier mâché can be a rather messy process, so remember to cover your work surface with newspaper before you begin. Use either ordinary newspaper or lightweight paper to make papier mâché.

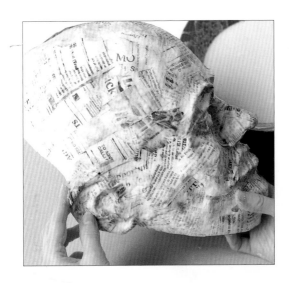

The Layering Method

◊ Tear the strips of paper into fairly small, evenly sized pieces.

◊ Mix a smooth paste from flour and water or use a proprietary wallpaper paste or a weak solution of PVA adhesive.

◊ So that you can be sure that you have completely covered the mask with each layer, either use different colours for each layer or lay the strips in different directions each time.

◊ Make sure that the previous layer is completely dry before you begin to apply the next layer.

◊ Do not put papier mâché near to a radiator or in front of a fire to dry – the paper will crack and twist out of shape. Leave it in a warm, dry room for about 2 hours.

The Pulp Method

Some of the masks – the Witch and the Punk, for example – involve the use of papier mâché pulp to build up the features. You can buy a proprietary pulp in many craft shops, but it is quite easy and much cheaper to make your own, especially as you will need only small amounts at a time.

◊ Tear newspaper into small pieces.

◊ Mix some paste and immerse the torn paper in it. Make sure all the pieces of paper are covered in the paste but do not allow them to become saturated.

◊ Squeeze the paste out of the paper and mould the pulp into shape. It will adhere easily to the surface of papier mâché.

◊ The pulp will take longer to dry than single layers of papier mâché, and it is best to leave it overnight if possible to make sure it is absolutely dry.

HOLDING THE MASKS IN PLACE

Elastic can be used to hold masks in place, but some of the more complicated masks, especially the Punk and Witch, need strong tape. Outsize masks, like the Monster, are best secured with strips of card that run over the top and around the back of the head.

◊ The simplest method is to fix tapes (either plastic or fabric) to the reverse side of the sides of the mask with strong adhesive tape.

◊ Make a small hole at each side of the mask and push string or elastic through the holes. Hold the elastic or string in place by tying neat knots on the right side so that they do not slide through the holes.

◊ Make a slit at each side of the mask and thread the tape through the slits from the back and use adhesive tape to hold the ends of the tapes securely at the back of the mask. The tapes emerge at the front so that they can be taken around to the back of the head and tied together.

◊ Use a small stick – the sticks sold in garden centres for propping up indoor plants are ideal – and uses adhesive tape to hold it securely to the back of the mask. This method means that the mask can be raised and lowered easily.

◊ Cut two strips of light-weight card, one to reach around the back of your head, and the second to reach from the top front of the mask to about halfway down your head so that it reaches the first piece. Check that the mask is comfortable and secure before stapling the strips to the edge of the mask and to each other.

FABRIC AND FEATHERS

The Panda Mask is made from fur fabric, which looks wonderfully appealing. Other masks could easily be made from scraps of left-over fabric so that you can use different colours and textures. Fur fabric is available from most craft shops and haberdashers, and it is easy to work with. There is no need to

stitch the pieces together – a clear adhesive or a special fabric adhesive will hold the material firmly together.

Feathers give a wonderfully sophisticated, rather exotic look to a mask. You can buy ready-dyed ones, but it is easy to colour feathers with ordinary cold water dye so that you could, for example, make a feathered mask to match a particular dress or outfit. Look in fishing equipment shops for some unusual feathers, as well as in craft suppliers.

Your local craft shop will also be a good source for a variety of beads, sequins and spangles that can be used in various ways to decorate masks. Even a simple half-mask can be enlivened by an edging of multi-coloured sequins.

SEASIDE SPECTACLES

This mask is fun to make and it should be fun to wear. We have used the outline of a fish, but you could use a starfish or crabs, for which we have included templates, or you could design your own spectacles, drawing your inspiration from anything you see on the seashore – shells or seaweed, for example. We decorated the mask with adhesive dots and coloured paper, but you could make it really spectacular by using beads or sequins.

You will need
◊ Medium-weight green card
◊ Pencil
◊ Tracing paper
◊ Scissors
◊ Hole punch
◊ Adhesive tape
◊ Medium-weight coloured paper
◊ Coloured adhesive dots
◊ Black felt-tip pen
◊ Clear, all-purpose adhesive
◊ Pinking shears

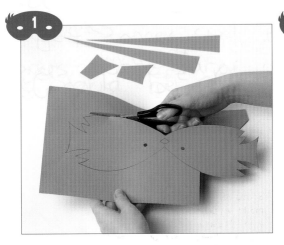

1 Trace the image of your choice and the side pieces from the template on page 45 onto medium-weight green card. Punch out the eye holes and then cut out the shape and the side pieces.

2 Turn over the shape and use adhesive tape to attach the side pieces.

3 Decorate the cut-out fins with strips of coloured paper and adhesive dots. Use a felt-tip pen to make some smaller spots in the centre of the dots.

4 Score along the narrow edge of each fin and fold them along the score line. Apply adhesive to the small flap and stick each fin in place on the front of the mask.

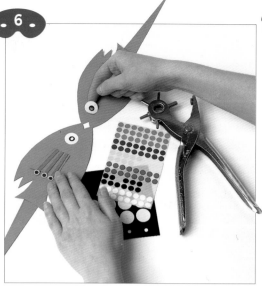

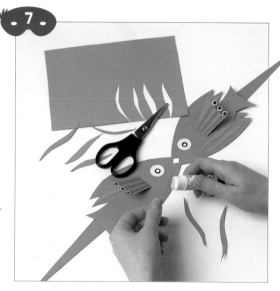

5 Place a small black adhesive dot in the centre of a large white dot and punch a hole through the centre.

6 Place this over one of the eye holes already made. Repeat for the other eye.

7 Cut some curved pieces from a piece of coloured paper – we used turquoise – and glue them in position, using the illustration as a guide.

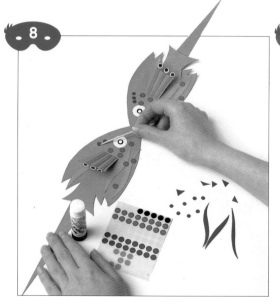

TIP

• You can buy adhesive dots – and other shapes – that are already coloured, but rather than buy packets of coloured ones that you may never use, buy white ones and paint them to match the other colours that you are using on your mask. Apply the paint before you peel the dot away from the backing sheet so that you can paint right up the edges of the circle. If you try to apply the paint once the dot is in place, you will find it difficult to paint it neatly without getting paint on the background colour.

8 Cut some more curved strips in a contrasting colour – we used dark blue – and glue them in place, together with some more coloured dots. You may find a wooden cocktail stick useful for pushing and pressing the small dots into place.

9 Cut some wedge-shaped pieces of light blue paper, using pinking shears to give a neatly jagged edge, and glue long triangles of dark blue paper down the centre of each piece.

10 Glue these blue pieces to the tails of the fish.

11 Finish off with some strips of yellow paper, cut into long, narrow wedge shapes, and glue them in position along the top edges of the fish.

HALF-MASK

This striking half-mask is easily made with medium-weight card, and it is coloured with pastels. We have included two templates, one for a man (page 48) and one for a woman (page 46), and you can use the basic design and method in many different ways, changing the hairstyle and the hat to give a completely different effect. Look through a library book to get some ideas from historical costumes, especially uniforms.

You will need
◊ Medium-weight card
◊ Pencil
◊ Tracing paper
◊ Scissors
◊ Coloured pastels
◊ Fixative
◊ Black crayon
◊ Scalpel
◊ Tape
◊ Adhesive tape
◊ 2 ostrich feathers

1 Transfer the outline of the template on page 48 to white card and cut around the outline.

2 Take a selection of flesh-coloured pastels and begin to shade in the face area. Blend the colours by rubbing them gently with a finger.

TIP

• Half-masks give only a partial disguise because the wearer's mouth and nose are still visible. Try to match the skin colour of the mask to the tones of the wearer's own skin.

3 Mark the eyebrows with brown pastel and use darker pink for the areas around the temples. Spray lightly with fixative.

4 Use several browns to colour the hair. Colour in the hat, using the illustration as a guide.

5 Cut out the eye holes with a scalpel, using a piece of spare paper over the mask so that you do not smudge the colours with your hand.

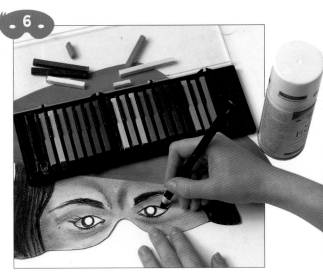

6 Colour in the area around the eye holes with black crayon and shade in the darker areas of the face. Finish the hair, lightly smudging the colour with your finger, then spray it with fixative.

7 Finish off the hat with random sweeps of orange.

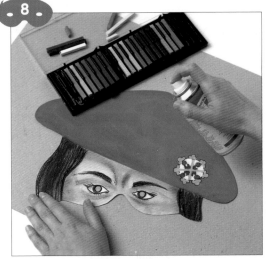

8 Spray the mask with fixative and leave to dry.

9 Use the scalpel to make tiny slits at the side of the mask in the hair area and push tape through to the back.

TIP

• We used black tape to tie on the mask because it is less obvious with dark hair. If you change the hair colour, use tape that matches the hair colour as closely as possible.

10 Turn over the mask and secure the tape with adhesive tape.

11 Tape two feathers together and put them in position. Attach them to the back of the mask with adhesive tape.

LION MASK

You will need paper, card and pastels for this mask, which is really fairly simple to make although it does look very impressive. It is quite time-consuming to complete because the lion's mane is made from individual strips of paper, and although it would be possible to make a less complicated version – a child could easily make the basic mask – the mane really does bring the mask to life.

You will need
◊ Medium-weight brown card
◊ Pencil
◊ Tracing paper
◊ Scissors
◊ Hole punch
◊ Pastels, including white, shades of brown and black
◊ Fixative
◊ Black crayon
◊ Medium-weight paper, four shades from brown to beige
◊ Light-weight white paper
◊ Clear, all-purpose adhesive
◊ Adhesive dots, black and yellow
◊ Tape or elastic

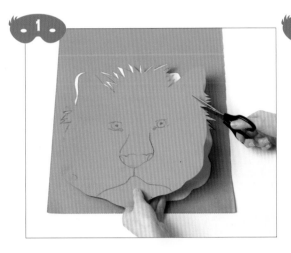

1 Transfer the outline from the template on page 47 to the brown card and cut out the shape.

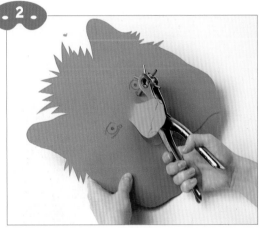

2 Cut around the nose area and punch out the eye holes (for you to see through).

3 Use a selection of brown, yellow and beige pastels to begin to colour in and shade the lion's face.

4 Use white to colour in around the mouth, eyes and eyebrows and rub the pastels carefully with your finger to blend the colours together. Spray with fixative and leave to dry.

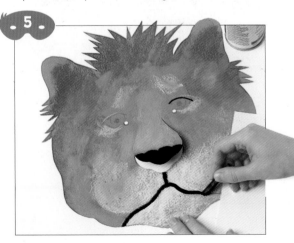

5 Use the black crayon to draw in the line of the mouth and the nostrils.

6 Protect the pastels you have applied by resting your hand on a piece of spare white paper while you work. Draw round the eyes with black crayon.

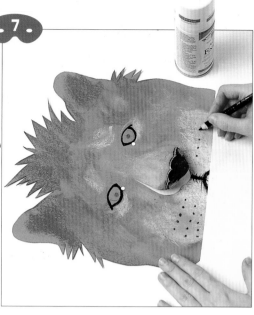

7 Make a series of small black dots on the cheeks and muzzle area, using the illustration as a guide. Spray again with fixative and leave to dry.

8 Cut out narrow strips of coloured paper for the top of the mane, shaping them into a point at one end.

9 Begin to glue the strips to the top of the mask to create the shape of the head, adding strips of paper in different shades of brown and yellow.

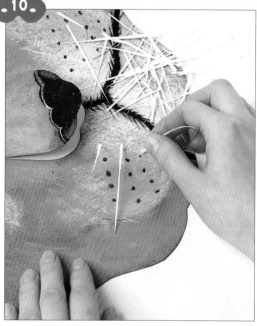

10 Cut out some strips of white paper for the whiskers on the muzzle and chin and glue them in place.

11 Cut some longer strips for the side of the mane.

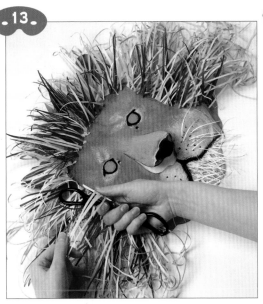

12 Cut some pieces for the mane from strips about 2.5cm (1in) wide. Do not cut all the way along the strips, but roll them up at the uncut end and glue them in place at the sides.

13 When the glue is dry, carefully run some of the strips of paper between the edge of the blade of a pair of scissors and your thumb to curl the paper slightly.

14 Put a black adhesive dot on a larger yellow dot for each eye and press them into position.

MEDUSA MASK

This mask is based on the legend of Medusa, a monster in Greek mythology whose hair was a mass of living snakes. This cardboard and paper mask requires a little patience to make, and you will also need to exercise your painting skills in decorating the face and applying the hair.

You will need
◊ Light-weight card
◊ Pencil
◊ Tracing paper
◊ Scalpel
◊ Scissors
◊ Clear, all-purpose adhesive
◊ Paints, including red, green and yellow
◊ Toothbrush
◊ Large and small paintbrushes
◊ White paper
◊ Black paper
◊ Adhesive tape
◊ Adhesive dots
◊ Hole punch

1 Transfer the outlines of the masks from the templates on page 47 and cut them out carefully from the card.

2 Use a scalpel to cut a slit in the mouth.

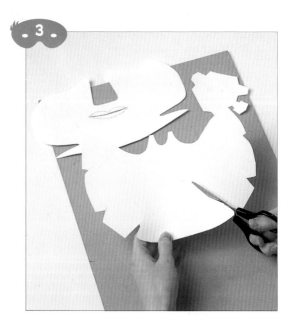

3 Cut along the lines indicated on the template and fold the top part of the mask into shape by overlapping the cut areas and gluing them together to create the three-dimensional effect.

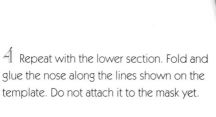

4 Repeat with the lower section. Fold and glue the nose along the lines shown on the template. Do not attach it to the mask yet.

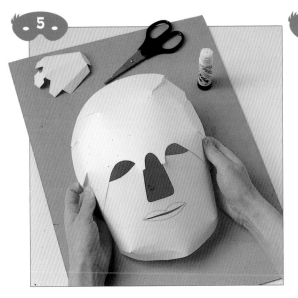

5 Fit the top section of the mask to the lower part and glue the two sections together. Leave to dry.

6 Mix some red paint and use an old toothbrush to spatter paint over the surface of the mask and the nose.

7 Mix green paint and repeat the process, this time using a large, soft paintbrush.

8 Mix some yellow paint and flick it over the mask and nose until you have built up a good covering of colour.

9 Make as many snakes as you need from light-weight white paper. Draw a rough free-hand circle and mark the outline of the snake with a pencil, using the template as a guide. Decorate them with different patterns and colours to create a variety of textures.

10 Cut out the snakes, using your pencil line as a guide, but do not make them all exactly the same.

11 Begin to glue the cut-out snakes to the front of the mask, twining them together to make them look as if they are alive. Try to not to put snakes that are the same colour next to each other, and leave a few heads and tails visible.

12 Use a fine paintbrush and white paint to add some final details to the snakes' heads and then paint in Medusa's eyebrows and the snakes' eyes in black or brown.

13 Paint in Medusa's mouth with dark red.

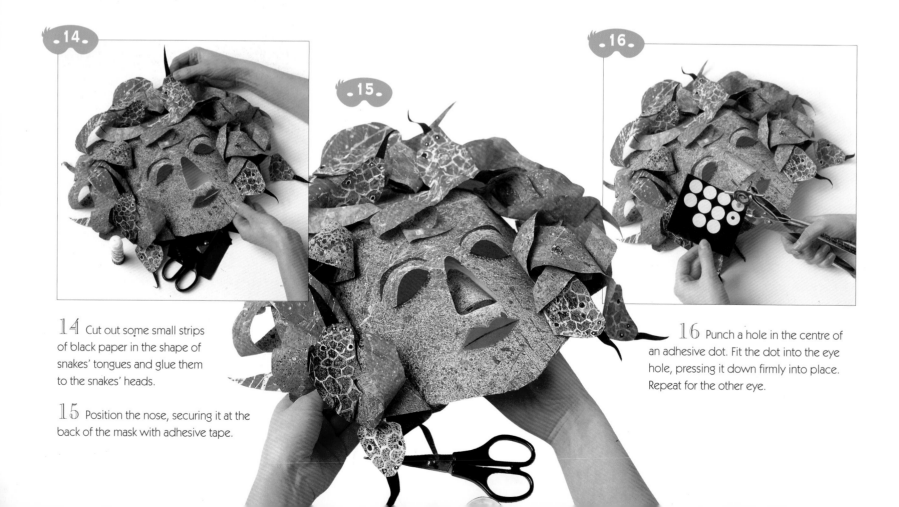

14 Cut out some small strips of black paper in the shape of snakes' tongues and glue them to the snakes' heads.

15 Position the nose, securing it at the back of the mask with adhesive tape.

16 Punch a hole in the centre of an adhesive dot. Fit the dot into the eye hole, pressing it down firmly into place. Repeat for the other eye.

WOODLAND HALF-MASK

This is the perfect mask for someone who enjoys walking in the countryside and picking up odd bits and pieces. The base is made of papier mâché, moulded on modelling clay, and it is decorated with leaves and berries. It is rather delicate, so handle it with care. Make sure that you use good quality gold, bronze and silver paints to give it a really sumptuous look.

You will need
◊ Pencil
◊ Tracing paper
◊ Light-weight card
◊ Modelling clay
◊ Newspaper and paste for papier mâché
◊ Scalpel
◊ Scissors
◊ Elastic
◊ Gold, silver and bronze spray paint
◊ Selection of dry leaves, berries, fruit and so on
◊ Clear, all-purpose adhesive

TIP

• If you do not like working with papier mâché or you do not have the time that is needed to model the mask, try decorating the basic shape of the Feathered Half-mask on page 26 –but remember to omit the beak.

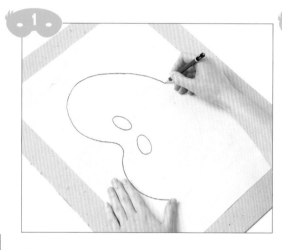

1 Trace the template on page 45 and transfer the image to a piece of card.

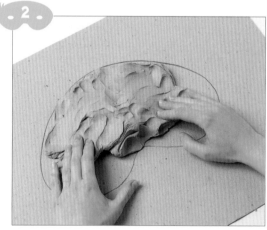

2 Use modelling clay to mould the shape on the card. Begin to build up a three-dimensional shape around the nose area, smoothing and refining the shape out towards the eyes.

3 Use the palms of your hands to smooth the clay and neaten the edges.

4 Take especial care to shape the nose and to smooth the clay around it, then leave the mould to dry for 24 hours.

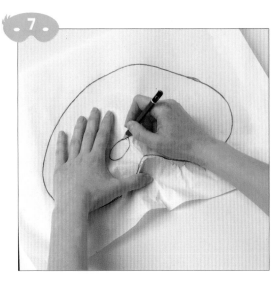

5 Mix the paste to an even consistency and use torn up scraps of newspaper, dipped in the paste, to cover the clay with a layer of papier mâché. Squeeze the strips with your fingers to remove excess paste from the paper before you press it in place or the papier mâché will take too long to dry.

6 Leave the mask in a warm place for 2–3 hours to dry, then repeat the process three more times – that is, you will apply a total of four layers of papier mâché. Leave the mask to dry completely, preferably overnight, before removing the mask from the mould.

7 Using the template as a guide, draw eye holes on the mask and cut them out carefully with a scalpel.

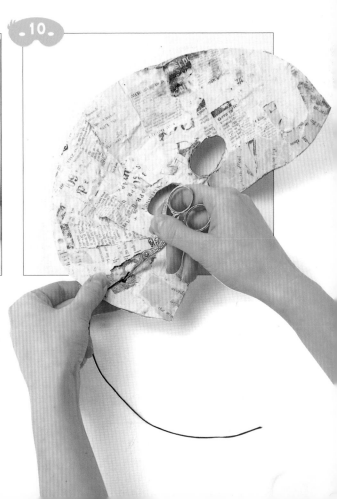

8 Trim the rough edges of the mask with scissors.

9 Use small pieces of papier mâché all around the edge to neaten it and to make a smooth line.

10 Make a small hole at each side and, from the back, push through the elastic, securing the ends with small knots.

11 Cover your work surface with newspaper or work outside and spray the mask evenly with gold paint.

12 Spray the leaves, berries, nuts and fruit with gold, silver or bronze paint and leave them to dry.

13 Begin to glue the leaves over the mask, using different colours and shapes to build up the overall shape. Finish off by adding the fruits, nuts and berries.

TIPS

• When you use spray paints, always work in a well-ventilated room – better still, work outside. You might prefer to use metallic paints that are applied by brush.

• Leaves should be preserved between paper and weighted down with books for one to two weeks before use.

PANDA

Fur fabric is ideal for animal masks – they always look so appealing. You can buy fur fabric in most haberdashery shops and in many craft shops, and it is easy to work with. The panda is very straightforward to make, and you could easily adapt the basic method to make almost any type of animal you want.

You will need
◊ Pencil
◊ Tracing paper
◊ Light-weight white card
◊ Scissors
◊ Hole punch
◊ Fur fabric, white and black
◊ Clear, all-purpose adhesive
◊ White pencil or French chalk
◊ Small, shallow yoghurt pot
◊ Buttons for eyes and nostrils

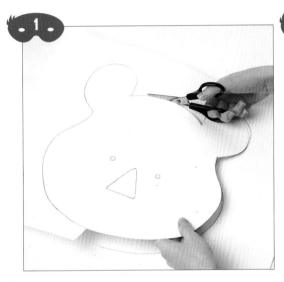

1 Transfer the outline from the template on page 46 to white card and cut it out.

2 Cut out the nose and punch out the eye holes.

3 Trace around the cardboard template onto the reverse side of the white fur fabric, but do not trace around the ears.

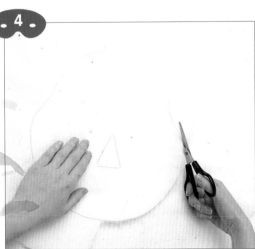

4 Cut out the outline of the head and cut out the nose hole.

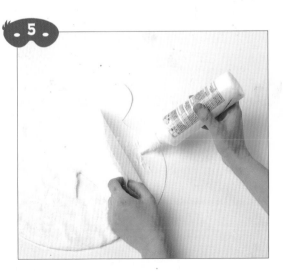

5 Glue the reverse side of the white fur fabric onto the cardboard template and leave the glue to dry.

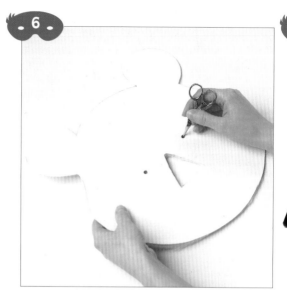

6 Pierce the eye hole with the sharp points of your scissors. Make sure you can see through the holes. You may have to trim some of the fur on the right side of the mask so that you can see clearly.

7 Cut out the templates for the ears, eye patches and nose, and draw them on the reverse side of the black fabric.

8 Cut the ears, eyes and nose patch from the black fabric.

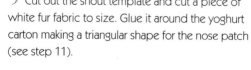

9 Cut out the snout template and cut a piece of white fur fabric to size. Glue it around the yoghurt carton making a triangular shape for the nose patch (see step 11).

10 Tuck the extra bits of white fur fabric into the yoghurt carton and glue them in position.

11 Glue the black nose piece, reverse side up, onto the end of the yoghurt carton.

12 Glue the eye and ear patches to the main mask. Make sure that you join the edges of the black and white neatly together.

13 Glue the nose into the middle of the mask between the black eye patches.

14 Stick on buttons for the eyes and nostrils and leave until the glue is dry.

FEATHERED HALF-MASK

This feathered half-mask is quite sophisticated, and it would look great with an evening dress. Feathers always make a mask look elegant and exotic, but they are easy and quick to use. Although we have used green and black feathers, you can buy dyed ones and, by changing the basic shape of the mask, you could make a parrot or a peacock or an owl – or almost anything else you wanted. You can also mount this kind of mask on a stick in case you do not want to wear it all evening.

You will need
◊ Black card
◊ Tracing paper
◊ Pencil
◊ White pencil or crayon
◊ Scissors
◊ Scalpel
◊ Clear, all-purpose adhesive
◊ Wooden cocktail stick
◊ Sequins
◊ Feathers, green and black
◊ Adhesive tape
◊ Black tape for tying

TIP

• Sequins can be fiddly to position. Look out for the kind that are sold stitched together in long strings. These are much easier than loose ones to stick in a straight line.

1 Draw the template image on page 46 onto tracing paper and go over the outline with a white pencil. Transfer this image to black card by pressing down firmly on the wrong side of the pencil line. The image should be clearly visible on the black card.

2 Cut out the mask and the two pieces of beak from the card. Score lightly along the length of the upper edge of both beak sections.

3 Cut a series of small incisions along the top edge of the beak, taking care that you do not cut beyond the score line. Bend along the score line carefully.

4 Apply a line of adhesive to the cut edges and press the two pieces together firmly to make the beak.

5 Decorate both sides of the edge of the beak with gold heart-shaped sequins. Use a wooden cocktail stick to help you position the sequins in an even line.

6 Glue the beak in position between the eye holes. Wait until the glue is dry. You may have to hold the beak in place for a few minutes until it is securely held in position.

7 Begin to stick the feathers around the mask, starting in the centre and working out to the side. Try to make the two sides as symmetrical as possible.

8 Turn over the mask and use strong adhesive tape to hold black tape near to the eye holes.

9 On the right side, use adhesive and the cocktail stick to stick multi-coloured, heart-shaped sequins onto the feathers.

10 Finish the mask by gluing a line of gold sequins around each eye hole.

FATHER CHRISTMAS

Paper plates make good bases for masks – they are cheap, readily available and easy to use. We have made a Father Christmas, but you could use the same method to make a pumpkin for a Halloween party or a snowman for a Christmas party, or a rag doll, a scarecrow, a football or even a clock. Even fairly young children can use this method, and you can use all kinds of different things to decorate them – so save all your odd scraps of material, beads, straw and felt.

You will need

◊ 4 Large paper plates
◊ Pencil
◊ Ruler
◊ Scissors
◊ Hole punch
◊ Scalpel
◊ Paints
◊ Large and small paintbrushes
◊ Adhesive dots
◊ Clear, all-purpose adhesive

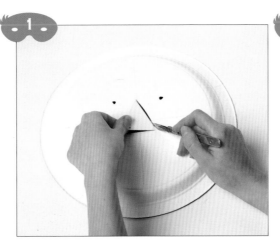

1 Use the template on page 48 and draw the nose and eye holes on a large paper plate. Punch out the eye holes and cut out the nose.

2 Cut out the separate nose section, fold it in half down the centre and paint it pink. Use the same paint to colour the plate pink. Draw two circles for the cheeks, and colour two adhesive dots with blue paint for the eyes.

3 Punch a hole in the middle of the adhesive dots and position them over the eye holes. Paint the cheeks red.

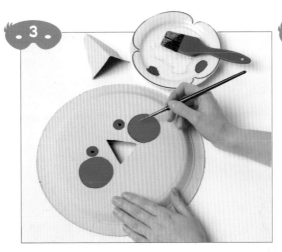

4 Glue the nose in position between the cheeks.

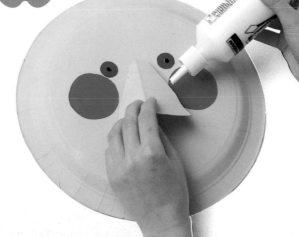

5 Using the template and illustrations as reference, cut the hair and moustache from a paper plate.

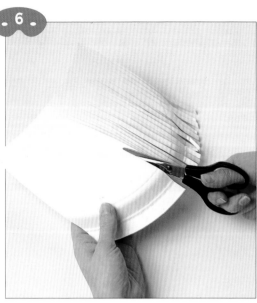

6 Cut the beard from another plate, making the separate strands as fine and even as you can.

7 Glue the fringe and moustache into place on the face, holding them until the glue is dry.

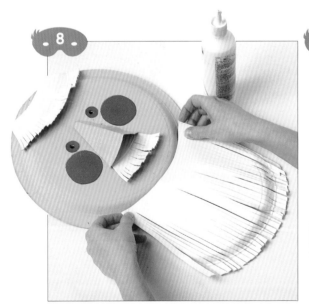

8 Glue the beard in place.

9 Glue on the hair in sections. There are three sections at each side, so begin with the lowest one, making sure they are placed symmetrically.

10 Cut out the hat and paint it red.

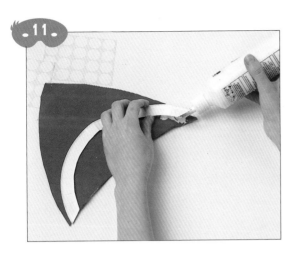

11 Cut out the semicircle for the decorative band on the hat and glue it into place.

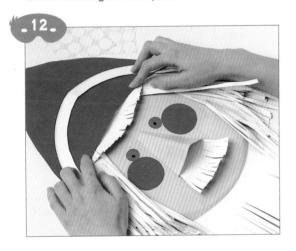

12 Glue the hat onto the main mask, holding it in place until the glue is dry.

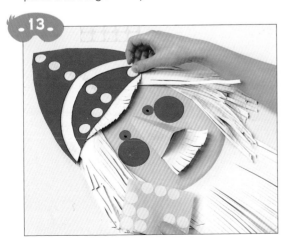

13 Decorate the hat with adhesive white dots.

WITCH

This is a traditional papier mâché mask, made on a balloon, which is one of the easiest and best ways of making a mask for a complete costume. It is the perfect mask for Halloween or for a fancy dress party. Although it is time-consuming to make, it offers great scope for you to use your imagination, both in making the facial features and in adding decorations to the hat.

You will need

◊ Balloon
◊ Newspaper and paste for papier mâché
◊ Modelling clay or Plasticine
◊ Scalpel or craft knife
◊ Scissors
◊ Black crayon or pencil
◊ Scalpel
◊ Paints
◊ Large and small paintbrushes
◊ Tape for tying
◊ Pencil or white crayon
◊ Length of string
◊ Drawing pin
◊ Heavy- or medium-weight black card
◊ Double-sided adhesive tape or clear, all-purpose adhesive
◊ Black raffia
◊ Adhesive tape
◊ Plastic lizards, newts, spiders and so on
◊ Silver net

1 Blow up the balloon to slightly larger than your head. Tear some newspaper into strips and dip the pieces into the paste, squeezing off the excess with your fingers. Cover about three-quarters of the balloon with pasted paper and leave it to dry.

2 Repeat the process twice more – that is, you apply three coats of papier mâché in all – and leave it to dry completely. Burst the balloon, remove the pieces and trim off the edges of the papier mâché.

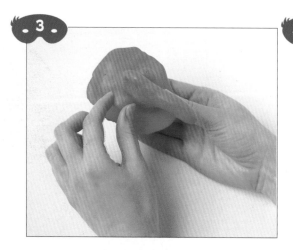

3 Use modelling clay or Plasticine to mould a nose. Add some small round balls to represent warts.

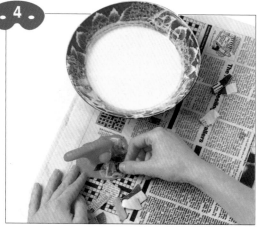

4 Tear some more, smaller strips of newspaper and cover the nose with papier mâché. Leave to dry. Apply another layer of papier mâché and leave to dry.

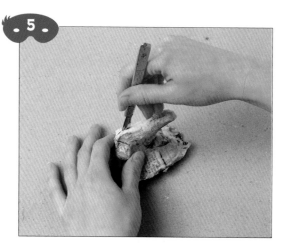

5 Cut the nose in half with a scalpel or craft knife. Carefully peel off the nose from the Plasticine, taking care that it does not tear.

6 Join the two halves of the papier mâché nose with small pieces of pasted paper.

7 Trim the edges of the nose carefully with scissors so that it will sit securely on the front of the mask.

8 Place the nose in the centre of the mask and hold it in place with small pieces of papier mâché. Leave it to dry.

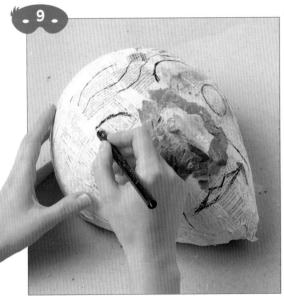

9 Draw on the face, eyebrows, cheeks and mouth with black pencil.

TIP

• When you make papier mâché, tear the paper into strips so that you do not have sharp, cut edges, which do not lie smoothly, and always tear the strips in the same direction.

10 Make a small amount of papier mâché pulp (see page 6) and build up the eyebrows, cheeks and chin. Leave to dry overnight.

11 Roll small pieces of newspaper and dip them in paste, sticking them on the mask to represent wrinkles and lines.

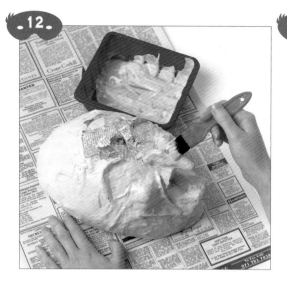

12 Paint the face all over with pale grey, making sure that you cover all the newsprint.

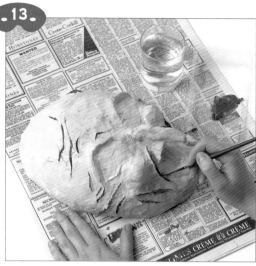

13 Use dark grey paint and a fine brush to paint all the wrinkles and lines.

14 Pierce the eye holes with the point of the scissors. Try on the mask at this stage to make sure you can see properly.

15 Begin painting the cheeks, nose, chin, eyes and so on with red and pink paint.

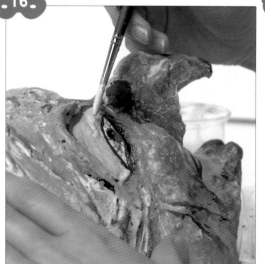

16 Use white to paint around the eyes and between the lips, and use a dark red to paint the lips and warts and to outline the eyes. Make the eyes themselves look bloodshot by painting in fine red lines. Paint the area below the eyebrows with pale pink.

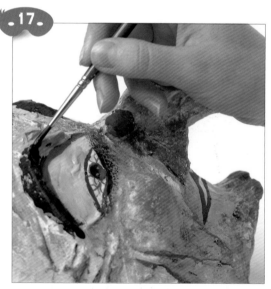

17 Use black paint for the eyebrows.

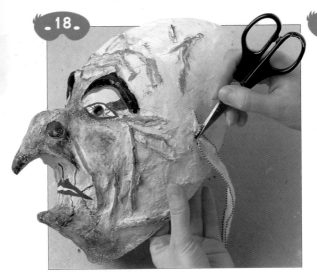

18 Pierce a hole on each side of the face with the point of your scissors. Push the tape through the hole and knot it on the inside to hold it secure.

19 To make the hat attach a piece of string to a pencil. Make a loop at the other end of the string and hold it in place with a drawing pin in the corner of the card. Keeping the string under tension, draw an arc onto the card that will make a cone large enough to make the witch's hat. Cut out the shape.

20 Use double-sided tape or adhesive to hold the long sides of the cone together.

21 Place the cone on a sheet of black card and use a white crayon to draw around the base.

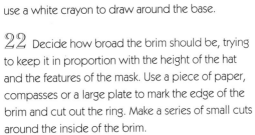

22 Decide how broad the brim should be, trying to keep it in proportion with the height of the hat and the features of the mask. Use a piece of paper, compasses or a large plate to mark the edge of the brim and cut out the ring. Make a series of small cuts around the inside of the brim.

23 Fold the cuts upwards and apply glue on the sides facing the rim.

24 Stick the crown of the hat onto the brim, making sure that the brim is firmly stuck to the crown.

25 Cut the black raffia to suitable lengths and use small pieces of adhesive tape to stick clumps of hair to the inside of the hat.

26 Glue the lizard, net and spider to the hat and leave to dry.

PUNK

Papier mâché masks always take a long time to make because you have to wait for the individual layers of pasted paper to dry. However, the results are so spectacular and impressive that it's always worth the effort. We decided to make this punk look fairly restrained and sculptural by applying a single colour, but you could use a range of colours to make the face look more – or less – sinister.

You will need
◊ Kitchen foil
◊ Scissors
◊ Newspaper and paste for papier mâché
◊ White paint
◊ Paintbrush
◊ Tracing paper
◊ Pencil
◊ Light-weight white paper
◊ Clear, all-purpose adhesive
◊ Wire for earrings, nose rings and so on
◊ Safety pins
◊ Chain, cross or other decorations
◊ Tape for tying

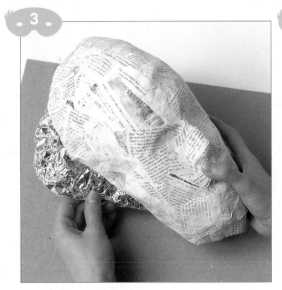

1 Take three sheets from a wide roll of kitchen foil and press them over your face so that you get a reasonable impression of your features. The mask will eventually fit under your chin and around over the top of your head, so make sure that you have enough foil to cover the whole area. You will need to press quite firmly around your nose, mouth and eyes.

2 Mix the paste to a smooth, even consistency and tear strips of paper. Dip the strips into the paste, removing the excess paste with your fingers. Take great care when you apply the pasted paper to the tin foil that you do not press it out of shape. Apply one layer of paper and leave to dry for 2–3 hours. When the first layer is dry, apply three more layers – that is, there are four layers of papier mâché in total – allowing each layer to dry before you apply the next.

3 Leave the final layer to dry overnight. When you are sure that the papier mâché is completely dry, carefully pull the tin foil away from the inside.

4 Make a small amount of papier mâché pulp (see page 6) and use it to build up the eyebrows and nose. Leave it to dry for at least 2 hours.

5 Roll small balls of papier mâché pulp and use them for the eyeballs, positioning them carefully on the mask. Leave to dry.

6 Use more papier mâché pulp for the lips, using the end of your scissors to shape them. Leave to dry.

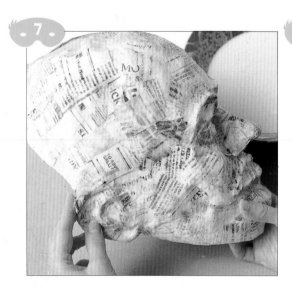

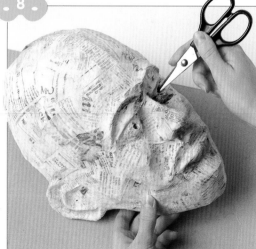

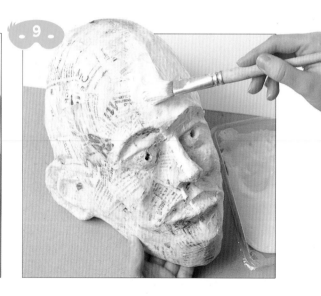

7 When you are satisfied with the shape of the lips, begin to build up the ears. You may need to look at yourself in the mirror as you work to position and shape them correctly. Leave the mask in a warm, dry place until it is absolutely dry. This can take 24 hours because pulp often takes longer than ordinary papier mâché to dry right through.

8 Make eye holes with the points of a pair of scissors then hold the mask to your face to make sure that you can see through the holes. Make two holes at the base of the nose so that you can breathe when the mask is over your head. Also make the holes at the sides through which the tapes for tying will be attached.

9 Paint the entire mask with white. You may need to apply two coats to cover the newsprint completely – remember to allow the first coat of paint to dry before you apply the second.

10 Cut out triangles of white paper and roll them up to make the hair spikes. It can be difficult to get the paper to roll just as you want, but persevere and you will soon get the knack.

11 Apply some glue to the inside edge of the paper so that it does not start to uncurl. Do not use stiff paper, which will not roll easily and will be difficult to keep in shape.

12 You will need to have smaller spikes for the front of the head, with larger ones towards the back. Cut the spikes so that they decrease in size gradually.

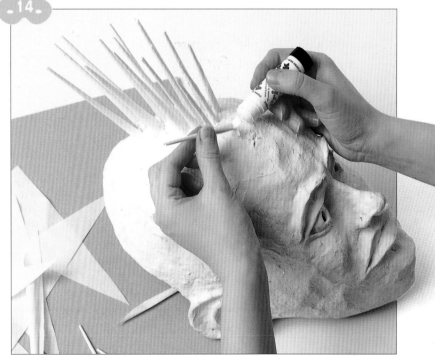

13 Snip the ends of the spikes in three places and pull the paper outwards a little so that there is a larger surface for gluing.

14 Apply adhesive to the cut ends and press each spike firmly down on the top of the mask. You may need to hold each spike in place until the glue begins to dry.

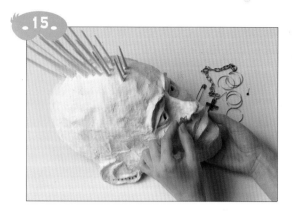

15 Use a sharp pin or needle to pierce holes in the nose as well as the ears.

16 Make earrings and nose rings from garden wire and push them through the holes.

17 Push a safety pin through one side of the nose, and take the chain and cross from one side of the nose to the ear. Push the tying tape through the holes at the sides and knot it on the inside to hold it secure.

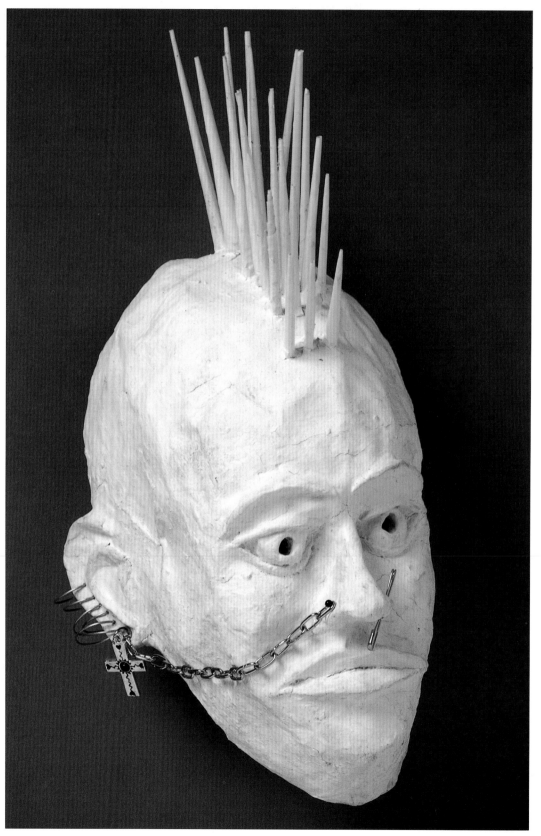

Monster Mask

This enviro-monster is made from recycled egg boxes – you will need the old moulded cardboard kind, not the newer clear plastic containers, and you will need a lot, so begin to collect them now. This mask costs very little to make and it would be a good holiday project. The basic method could be used with all kinds of recycled containers – boxes, cartons and even bottles – to make some really frightening monsters.

You will need
◊ Egg cartons
◊ Scissors
◊ Stapler
◊ Large and small polystyrene balls
◊ Clear, all-purpose adhesive
◊ Paint, including green, yellow and red
◊ Large and small paintbrushes
◊ Florist's wire
◊ Pliers
◊ Adhesive dots
◊ Light-weight white paper
◊ Paste
◊ Newspaper
◊ Adhesive tape
◊ Red paper
◊ Strips of light-weight card

1 Separate the individual containers from the cartons – they should pull apart quite easily – then staple them together into the shape of a face.

2 Glue small polystyrene balls between the sections, especially if there are any holes. You can buy polystyrene balls in various sizes in craft and haberdashery shops. Remember to leave eye holes.

3 Mix a murky green and paint the mask all over. Leave to dry.

4 Mix some yellow paint and apply it to parts of the mask to create some interesting highlights – or to look like slime.

= 41 =

5 Take two large polystyrene balls and push a length of florist's wire (stub wires) into and through each ball. Florist's wire is available in craft shops and flower shops. Use pliers or, if they are strong enough, your fingers to bend over the top of the wire, then pull the wire down so that the hook is caught securely in the top of the ball.

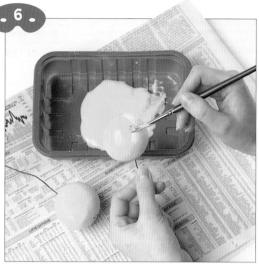

6 Hold the wires while you paint both balls yellow. Leave them to dry.

7 Mix some red paint and use a fine brush to paint red lines representing veins on the balls.

8 Paint two large adhesive dots with the same red and place them in the centre of the balls, over the end of the wire hook.

9 Push the wires through the mask so that the eyes are positioned where you want them, then twist the wires around on the inside of the mask to hold the eyes securely. Cut off any excess wire and cover the cut ends with adhesive tape. Try on the mask to make sure that you can see through it.

10 Make some whiskers by tearing white paper into long strips. Twist the strips and dip them into the paste so that they will retain their shape. Leave them to dry.

11 When the paste is dry, paint the whiskers – we chose grey, but you can use any colour you wish.

12 Use the points of your scissors to make a series of closely spaced, small holes at the sides of the mask. Thread the whiskers through the holes, adding a spot of glue to hold them in place if you want to.

13 Make the fangs from strips of newspaper, twisted into shape and dipped into paste. You will probably find it easier to make the fangs nicely pointed when they have been dipped in the paste, and while they are wet curve them slightly.

14 Leave the fangs to dry, then paint them, using the red and yellow paints to mix orange for the tips.

15 When the paint is dry, glue the fangs to a strip torn from an egg box, curving it slightly so that it fits along the bottom of the mask.

16 Use glue or adhesive tape to attach the row of fangs to the bottom inside edge of the mask.

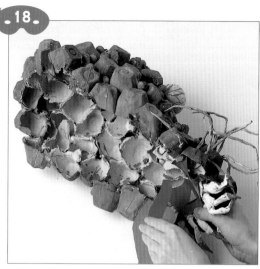

17 Tear a tongue shape from red paper or colour white paper with red paint.

18 Tape the tongue to the mask so that, from the front, it appears to be behind the fangs.

19 Staple strips of card to the back of the mask, trying it on to make sure that the strips will hold the mask securely but not too tightly over your face.

TEMPLATES

For reasons of space, the templates shown here are reproduced at half actual size. Before you can begin work you will need to enlarge the outlines.

The easiest method of enlarging is, of course, by photocopying. Many libraries, stationers and office equipment shops have photocopiers with an enlargement facility. Even if the photocopier cannot make a direct enlargement to twice the original size, you can usually enlarge the enlargement until you have the necessary dimensions.

If you do not have access to a photocopier, use the grid method. Use a sharp pencil and a ruler to draw a series of equally spaced lines across and down the original template. Try to surround the curved edges with the edges of a square or rectangle so that the edges of the shape just touch the straight edges. Take a large, clean sheet of paper or card and draw on it a square or rectangle that is twice as large as the original. Then cover this with vertical and horizontal lines that are spaced at twice

the distance of your first grid. For example, if the original squares were 2.5cm (1in) on the original, you would draw squares of 5cm (2in). If the pattern is complicated you will probably find it easier to have a small grid, say 1cm (⅛in), on the original and 2cm (1in) on the enlarged version. Transfer the shapes that are visible in each small square to the corresponding larger square on the new grid. If necessary, go over the outlines with a black felt-tip pen.

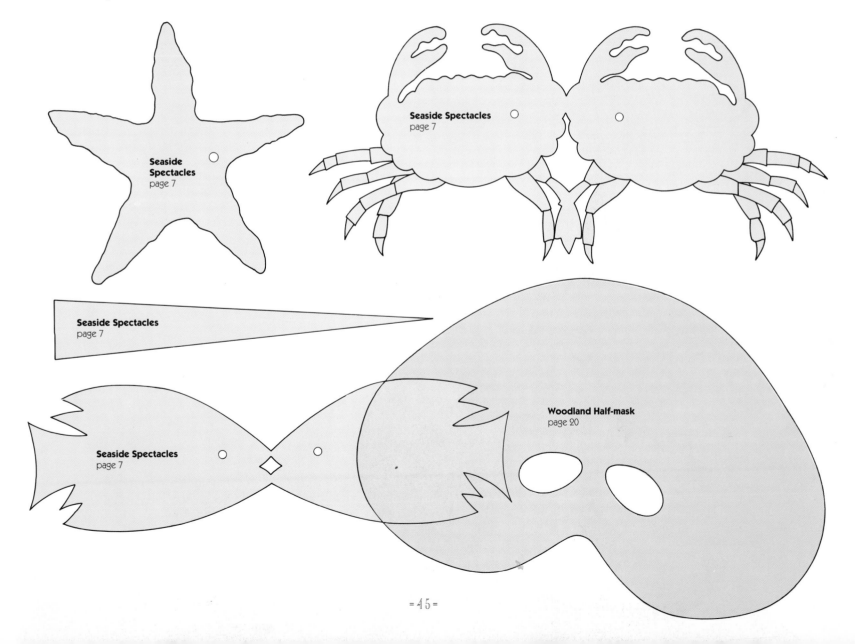

Seaside Spectacles
page 7

Seaside Spectacles
page 7

Seaside Spectacles
page 7

Seaside Spectacles
page 7

Woodland Half-mask
page 20

Panda
page 23

Panda
page 23

Panda
page 23

Feathered Half-mask
page 26

Feathered Half-mask
page 26

Feathered Half-mask
page 26

Half-mask (woman)
page 10

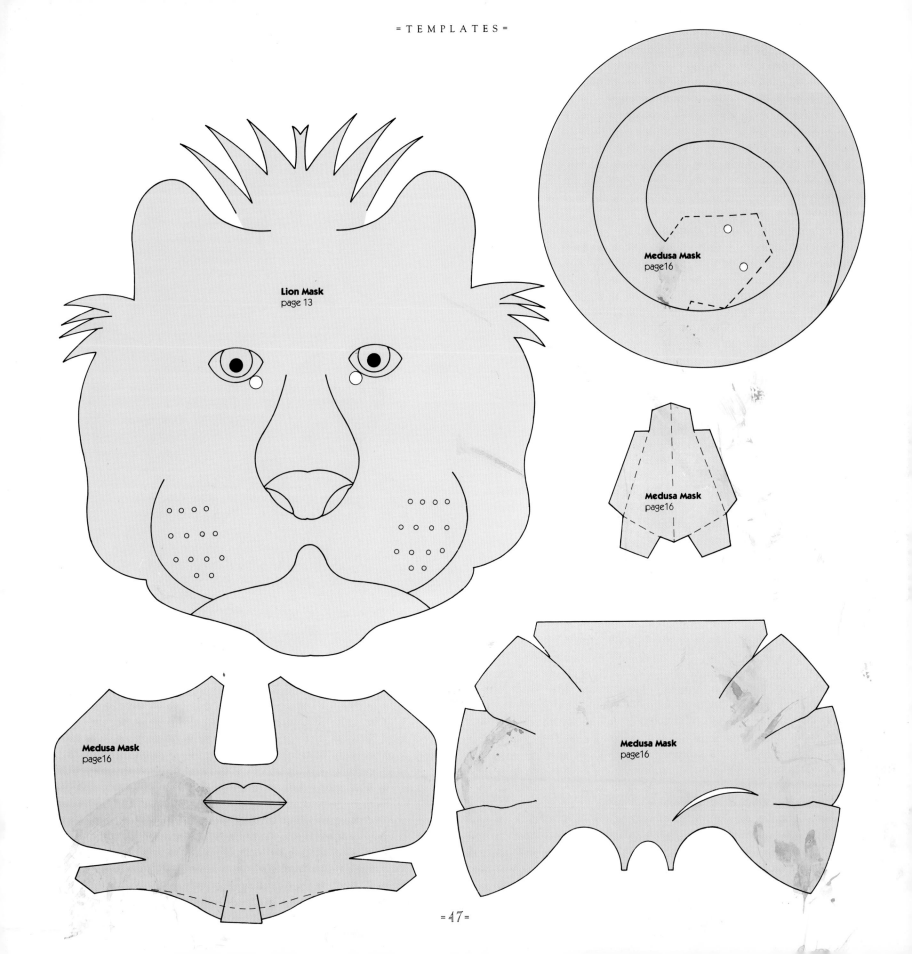

Lion Mask
page 13

Medusa Mask
page16

Medusa Mask
page16

Medusa Mask
page16

Medusa Mask
page16

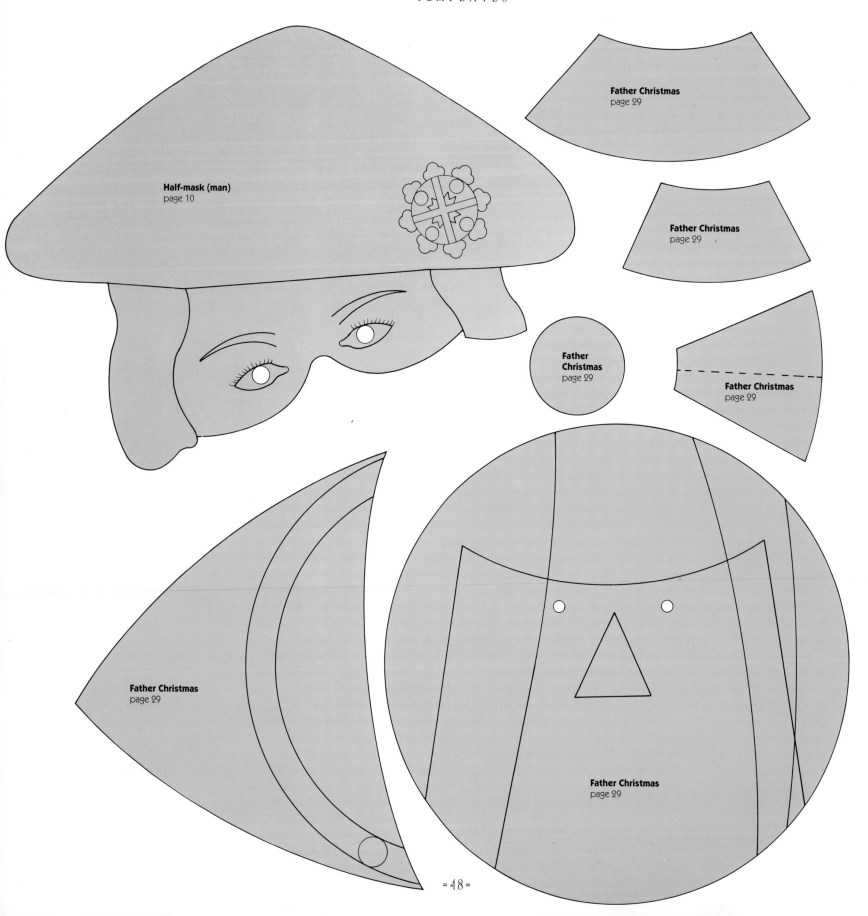

Father Christmas
page 29

Father Christmas
page 29

Half-mask (man)
page 10

Father Christmas
page 29

Father Christmas
page 29

Father Christmas
page 29

Father Christmas
page 29

Father Christmas
page 29